NOT FOR SALE

Cornelius Lindsey

ISBN 978-0-9912913-0-4 (paperback edition)

ISBN 978-0-9912913-1-1 (digital edition)

For information regarding special discounts for bulk purchases,
please contact info@corneliuslindsey.com.

Dedication

I would like to dedicate this book to anyone who has experienced the bondage of sin. It is my prayer that you are set free.

Table of Contents

The Price and Purchase

You are not a lost cause or a mistake.

You are not an accident.

You are not the derogatory names people have called or labeled you.

You are not a cheap, worthless, dirty rag.

You are special to God, and He paid a very hefty price for you.

Let's discuss the price and the purchase.

Without the shedding of the Blood of Jesus Christ, we would still be held in bondage to sin. We would have no way of escaping its grasp. We would be without hope and left for destruction. But, because of the shedding of His Blood, salvation is made possible for us. Hebrews 9:22 reads *"Almost all things are by the law purged with blood; and without shedding of blood is no remission."* It is difficult to deny the significance of the shedding of the Blood to the authors of the Bible. Matthew 26:28 reads, *"and not through the blood of goats and calves, but through His own blood, [Jesus] entered the holy place once for all, having obtained eternal redemption."* How can we ignore such truth? We have to see that it is important and essential.

When you study and compare Christianity with all the other religions in the world, you will see that Christianity has something that all the others lack—a Savior. This is what distinguishes the Christian faith from all the others religions and philosophies in the world. Christ paid the penalty for our sins by shedding His Blood on the cross as a sacrifice. He did not offer up a lamb in His place. Instead, He became the Lamb capable of paying the heavy price of our sin. He did what we could not do so we could share in what we do not deserve.

Now, how does Jesus's atoning sacrifice affect you? Why is understanding what Jesus did important for you and your life? To put it simply, you can now be reconciled to the Father because of the shedding of the Blood of the Son. Christ becomes your mediator, and there is no other sacrifice needed. A mediator is someone who speaks to another on your behalf. Jesus speaks to God about our sin because we cannot do it for ourselves. He is the reason the Father forgives us.

Because of Christ, guilt has been extinguished, reconciliation has been made possible, the final blood sacrifice has been given, and the possibility of salvation is made available. The way you receive this salvation is to join in union with this truth by faith. You must recognize that there is only one Savior, and He is Jesus—the hope of all mankind and God incarnate.

This should give you a reason to rejoice!

What the Father and Jesus accomplished on the Cross cannot be compared to anything else. It is special and holy.

> *"...having foreordained us unto adoption as sons*
> *through Jesus Christ unto himself, according to the*
> *good pleasure of his will, to the praise of the glory of*
> *his grace, which he freely bestowed on us in the*
> *Beloved: in whom we have our redemption through*
> *his blood, the forgiveness of our trespasses, according*
> *to the riches of his grace..."*
> (Ephesians 1:5-7)

Throughout Scripture, we see that there is no other way to be saved except through faith in Jesus Christ. Without Jesus, there is no hope, and eternal life would be far off. Because of Him we are forgiven, our sins are taken away and we are strengthened to abstain from future sin.

You have the choice of accepting Jesus Christ as the Lord of your life and begin to follow His Word as it is written. Or, you can deny the truth and inherit eternal damnation in hell. Do not reject the only hope there is for eternal life. If you reject this hope, there is no other source of hope remaining for you. Christ is not one of many options. He is the only option. He is unique. He stands alone in Himself, and He will not be denied. Which will it be for you: the Kingdom of Heaven or hell?

I bet you are probably thinking: Cornelius, I thought this was going to be a book about how special and great I am. I thought it was going to be a book of encouragement and hope. Where are those words? Honestly, there is no greater message of hope I can offer to you other than the Gospel. It is only by Christ that you can be set free from bondage and able to escape eternal damnation. Consider the length of eternity, and ask yourself if your trivial, earthly escapades are worth it. Are you sure that you want to gamble your eternity for a few moments of sinful indulgence? Is that boyfriend or girlfriend worth it? Is the influence of your friends worth it? Is the pursuit of money worth it? Are all the things we build up and allow to become idols worth an eternity in the lake of fire? Why even consider another option when Christ is all you will ever need? He did not just pay the price; He became the price for you and me. This is another opportunity for you to rejoice.

The price for saving us was not cheap, but it was definitely necessary. The only method of payment was by blood. The blood of animals could not fully pay the entire cost. The blood of a lamb could not be used to fulfill the entire bill; however, the blood of the Lamb was sufficient. It was there on the Cross that His precious blood was spilt for our sake. If we forsake or ignore the price we reveal how little we understand what was done for us. In the end we will forever diminish the precious nature of purchase.

Consider this, Christ purchased us with His blood. *"Be on guard for yourselves and for all the flock, among which the Holy Spirit has made you overseers, to shepherd the church of God which He purchased with His own blood."* (Acts 20:28) That word "purchased" is also used in 1 Timothy 3:13 in reference to the office of a deacon. It literally means "to acquire or gain anything; to make it ours." Christ did not go to Calvary to bargain for our ransom. The action on Calvary was an acquisition. It was a transaction. We have been obtained by acquisition unto salvation. He obtained or acquired the Church for Himself by paying with His own life. It was not the blood of some vagrant. A pure, innocent man paid the price. And by that payment, we were purchased.

I want you to consider a purchase. Let's say that I go to a store and purchase a radio. In order for me to purchase the radio, I must first have the capital to afford it, and I must use the capital to barter or exchange for the radio. I give the clerk $50, and the clerk gives me the radio. Now, here is an important question to consider: Who owns the radio after I purchased it? I do, right? I own the radio because I purchased it. I paid for it! I bought it! It belongs to me! Since it is mine, I have the right to do with it whatever I please. If someone wants my radio, he has 3 options. He can steal it from me, ask me for it, or try to buy it from me. Keep this in mind as we consider the next portion.

Consider the price Christ paid for you. I want you to reconsider the purchase. Christ acquired you. That means that you now belong to Him. Unlike the radio, there is not an affixed monetary price on you. He acquired you with something that money cannot buy. He did not pay just any price; He paid the ultimate price in this acquisition.

Now, let's say that the enemy decides to go to the Purchaser, which is Christ, and demands ownership of the property. Notice that the enemy cannot assume control on his own. He must approach the rightful owner. The enemy will do all he can to steal you away by deception and perversion. He already knows that Christ will not give you back to the bondage of sin. He will not hand over those who truly abide in Him. Christ will not release you back into sin's grasp. The enemy's last option is to try to bargain or barter for you. He must go to Christ to purchase you back from Him. In order to bargain or barter for you, the enemy must assume, determine and affix a price on you. For example, the radio in my example above was $50. In order to barter or bargain for the radio I must present something that is equal to the value of the radio. The enemy does not have anything of true value to offer for you. All he has is temptation to try and entice you back into the sin you have already been set free from through Christ. He must find a way to convince you to run back to the sin you once loved. All he is trying to do is figure out how much it will cost to seduce your soul unto damnation. So, how much are you worth? What sin is the enemy using to barter you back to damnation?

Follow me through this example as I clarify what we are talking about. There was a person who went up to a stranger and asked, "Can I sleep with you $100,000.00?" The stranger replied, "Umm, that sounds fine to me." "Well, how about $10.00? Can I sleep with you for $10?" In anger, the stranger replied, "How dare you! What kind of person do you take me for? What kind of person do you think I am?" The person responds saying, "We both know what kind of person you are. Now we are just agreeing on price."

Once the stranger agreed to sleep with the person for $100,000.00, it was evident that she or he had a price. All he needed to do was settle on the right price. Now, let me ask you this important question: What is your price? I want you to think about it as you read this book. Think about all the things that have been used to try to purchase you back. Think about all the deception and twisted Scripture that is been thrown your way to try to thwart you off the path of righteousness. Remember that if you have a price, you better believe that someone is going to try to buy you. My hope is that you realize you are not for sale as a prostitute to sin!

Prostitution

Prostitution is the exchange of sexual services by one person to another person in return for payment. The person who offers the sexual favor is a prostitute. While we recognize that prostitution is on the rise all over the world, we should realize that the sale of sexual favors is a longstanding profession that spans regimes, kingdoms, countries and centuries.

There are many advocacy groups who are trying to eliminate the structures that feed the enterprise of prostitution. Then, there are some who consider it legal and even acceptable. As difficult as it is to admit prostitution also makes up some of our Biblical history. Gomer, Hosea's wife, was a prostitute. Hosea married her when God told him to marry an unfaithful wife. Prostitution is not something new. It has been around for ages.

I have driven streets where I have seen men, women, boys and girls advertising their body for sex. Sadly, many of the prostitutes I have seen have been just a couple blocks away from a church building. Many of them were so disheveled. They looked like life was being sucked out of them as each second passed. When I saw them I was not at a place in my Christian walk where I wanted to walk up and offer any kind of assistance. My focus was on myself, not others. I did not have compassion for them. I just wanted my life to be in perfect order. I look back and I regret the opportunities I missed to minister to those in need because of my pride. I pray you will not squander those opportunities as they present themselves. Thankfully, I have received more of them in my life. Nevertheless, the image of those who are hurting and lost is so heartbreaking. It is clear what they are doing is wrong on so many levels, but many of them do not know it. Many of them are trying to make a living, trying to survive, and some are enslaved into the system. I have known organizations that have been started to go out in the streets to rescue those prostitutes. We can be passionate about taking them off the streets, but we must be even more passionate about renewing their minds. They must learn and understand to take the streets out of their own hearts. They must turn away from the rugged, ghetto mentally that secludes them from the commonwealth of purity and wholeness in Christ. It is not enough to tell them they are beautiful or try to increase their self-awareness. We must direct them back to Christ over and over and over again.

The goal here is not to heighten our awareness of sex and lust as if it is a greater sin than a lie. It is important to note that kingdoms, countries, homes, and marriages have been destroyed and ruined due to sexual immorality. Kings, presidents, prime ministers, preachers, pastors, statesmen, and other individuals of influence and power have been ruined due to sexual immorality. It seems like there is a new story every day about someone who was caught in some scandal because of a moral failure of a sexual nature. Such an offense tarnishes his or her name, bringing dishonor to his or her family and possibly destroy his or her marriage and home.

I was stung to the heart when I made the connection between what I saw prostitutes doing in the streets and what I was doing in the privacy of my own home. I would look down on them as if their situation was far worse than mine. While they were publicly selling their bodies, I was selling mine privately. No, I was not exchanging my body for money. I was doing something far worse in my opinion. I was selling my mind by watching pornography and continuing to indulge in perversion in the privacy of my own home. Although I was not on the streets, it was clear that the streets were in me. I had a perverted mentality that cut me off from the commonwealth of purity in Christ. I was not trying to abstain from sexual gratification. I was just becoming more of a professional at hiding it from everyone else. I did not want others to know about my sexual escapades. Honestly, I knew what I was doing was wrong, and I wanted someone to come along to tell me what I was doing was wrong. I heard the words of the preacher on Sunday morning when he said it was wrong. But, as I heard him say it over and over again I was becoming immune to those words to the point I did not fully believe him. I read the words in Scripture, but I did not have a true respect for God's word to follow it. I heard people say they were set free, but I did not really believe them. And honestly, I was not struggling with lust; I was fully giving in to it over and over again. I was not fighting; I was caving in time and time again. Pride became the legs I stood on so I could continue in my sexual indulgence. I was a prostitute to sin. I sold myself time and time again to it. And it was not just lust. I would lie, steal and commit other sinful acts. I am still working on many of those things today. I am not perfect. I have a way to go, but I am thankful I am not where I used to be doing many of things I used to do.

Remember that a prostitute has to make an exchange in order for the transaction to be complete. For example, someone could exchange his body for drugs. Usually, the exchange has to be equal to the value of the product that is being exchanged. Follow me here. For him to exchange his body for drugs means the amount of drugs is equal to the worth of his body. Let us say that the person traded his body for money. He is basically saying that is body is worth the agreed-upon monetary amount for the agreed-upon sexual act. Let us turn the attention back on you—

yes, you. How much are you worth in exchange for a sinful act? How much would it take for you to tell a lie? How much would it take for you to rob someone else? How much would it take for you to commit adultery? How much is the sin worth in comparison to what you are worth? I will tell you that the sin is worth eternity in hell. There is no exchange that is worth that steep a price. Do not be fooled. Do not exchange your body, mind or soul for sin. It is not worth it in the end. It is deadly. It robs you of peace and joy. It destroys your life time and time again.

If you have been prostituting yourself to sin, repent today. Repent right now. Confess your sins to the Lord. Say out loud that you are a sinner who has been convicted of the sin you have committed. Make sure you truly believe it in your heart. After confessing your sin, receive Christ as your Savior. Crown Him Lord of your life. Make a new commitment right here and right now to live for Him. Make a commitment to never sell yourself out to the highest bidder again. We have a promise from Jesus that He would not leave us helpless. After receiving Him, we are blessed with the presence of the Holy Spirit. He will help lead and guide you in all truth. He will teach you what you do not know. He will take you where you have been too afraid to go. He will comfort you in those tough moments. He will be your strength in those intense moments of temptation. Trust Him.

Live out your relationship with Him publicly so others see it. Be an example for your family and friends. You are no longer for sale to this world now that you realize you have been bought with a special price through Jesus Christ.

I want to make sure you grasp the seriousness of your worth. In the next chapter we will discuss who God appraises your worth.

The Appraisal

When I am getting an appraisal, I am searching for the estimated value of a certain item. I am judging the nature of something or someone so I can properly assess the quality or importance of what I am looking to attain.

Usually, there is an appraiser who is tasked with assigning a value to the item. In this situation, I am not focusing so much on objects as much as I am you. The various items around us hold very little value when we consider that they will all be destroyed one day. You can build the largest house in the neighborhood, but it does not mean it will stand forever. Sooner or later, the property value will depreciate if the owner fails to maintain the quality of the home. If the owner abandons it or allows certain external forces to destroy it, he or she will be at a loss. This is why it is important for the owner to properly care for the property. Caring for the property will increase the possibilities for the value to appreciate over time. Assuming that the owner performs regular maintenance on the property, it is safe to predict that the property will yield a profit when the time comes to sell. I think we all would agree with the following statement: we care for things we value.

Now we will insert you into this equation. I want you to grab your Bible, and turn to 1 Corinthians 6:19. I would prefer you see it instead of just reading it here in this book. Take this time to grab your Bible, please. After looking at it, I want you to consider what the apostle Paul wrote there. The verse reads, "Or do you not know that your body is a temple of the Holy Spirit who is in you, whom you have from God, and that you are not your own?" That is a powerful verse! Lets break it apart.

Initially, we notice that the verse directly references the body, and it clearly equates the body to a temple. A temple is not your typical edifice. It is not a place where just anything is permitted. A temple is not a bathroom in that it is not meant to take deposits of waste. It is not a playhouse where anyone can have their way inside. It is a special, dedicated building prepared and designed for worship. Consider Jesus' reaction when He learned that merchants were selling worldly merchandise in the temple (Matthew 21:12). He does not take too kindly to the temple being disgraced by the moneychangers. So what does he do? He immediately clears the temple of the merchandise and the sellers. He restores the sacredness back to the temple!

Consider your own body, what the apostle Paul calls the temple of the Holy Spirit. Since your body is where He resides, would it not make sense for it to remain holy just as He is holy?

If there is anything that grieves the Holy Spirit, it must be discarded, broken, and cast away. It cannot stand in His holy place where He resides. Are there some tables that need to be overturned in you life? Are there some things that need to be cleansed in you mind? If so, you must know that the Blood of Christ is the perfect solvent to clean out what is wrong. God's Spirit will not take residence just anywhere. The lodging must be holy and pure, and such cleansing cannot be accomplished solely by our works. It is done by the powerful work of Christ. However, as we become mature stewards, we grow in our understanding of what it takes to properly maintain the temple. We make sure we are up on all the maintenance. We seek to take the utmost care of the temple, not because it is ours, but because it is valuable to God.

Recognizing that the body belongs to God is a very important initial step in understanding its value. God would never seek to inhabit a depreciating, decaying edifice unless His goal was to rebuild it for His own glory and honor. Because He is holy, the temple He resides must be holy! There are no exceptions. Complete and total holiness is the costly price tag that cannot be attributed to worldly things. It far exceeds earthly currency because holiness is a defining characteristics of God's nature. God is holy. It is not merely one of His attributes. It is who He is.

Holiness is invaluable and priceless because God is invaluable and priceless. If His temple is to be holy, then that can only mean that His temple is priceless and invaluable. The place where God's Spirit dwells takes on the nature of God Himself. Therefore, the holy, priceless nature of God transforms the temple, or the body, into a place of holiness that far exceeds any price one would try to offer for it. And, you can rest assured the value does not depreciate unless God no longer inhabits the temple. If God is denied entrance, the temple will be ruined and discarded! Since God is eternal, you can take rest in knowing that the value of the body, or the temple, will be eternal as well!

You are not a piece of meat for sale at a second-rate store. If God's Spirit has taken residence within you, then your value has increased far beyond any person's worldly appraisal! Do not allow someone who does not have a license to appraise your temple. And I can ensure you that Christ is perfectly qualified to do the job. Do not give in to sexual immorality because you recognize that your body is God's House, not your own!

So, how much do you think you are worth? How much can someone buy you for? Are you a cheap sale? Can someone purchase you with smooth words and six-pack abs? Can a picture of breasts and long legs cause you to taint the holiness of God's temple? What is it? How much can someone pay to buy you? Is it a dollar? Are you worth a dollar? How about ten thousand dollars? How about a million dollars? How much are you really worth? Once you can answer that question truthfully considering all we have discussed in this chapter, I pray you begin to start living like it. If you are like me you will notice you have been selling yourself for cheap. It is time for some real change to take place. If we are going to make changes, we must discuss what needs to be changed and what that change should look like.

Change:
From What? To What?

We have heard so much about change in this young century. It has been a promise of man since his inception. Many have desired change in some area of his or her life. Leaders have promised change throughout history. Promising change is one thing; effectively communicating it is another. In order to proclaim the necessity of change we must clearly identify what needs to be changed and the process to changing it. So yes, we know change is necessary, but the questions we must ask are: Change; from what? To what?

FROM WHAT?

Our society dictates a standard that says, "Do as I say rather than what I do." Our actions do not match our words so our credibility is lost, witness is destroyed and ambassadorship is undermined. Our actions are important because they identify the substance of the heart. Matthew 7:15-20 reads, "Beware of the false prophets, who come to you in sheep's clothing, but inwardly are ravenous wolves. You will know them by their fruits. Grapes are not gathered from thorn bushes nor figs from thistles, are they? So every good tree bears good fruit, but the bad tree bears bad fruit. Every tree that does not bear good fruit is cut down and thrown into the fire. So then, you will know them by their fruits." Our actions, although wicked and perverse, are only the fruit on the tree. They are important to assist in classifying the tree and they help to determine the substance or nature of the root. You cannot kill the tree by destroying the fruit; you must pluck it up by the root. Like the fruit and the tree, our actions cannot be stopped or transformed by merely stopping them by willpower. We do not have sufficient power within ourselves to ward off all the temptations to sin that we are faced with. There must be a change in the heart.

The problem is that we are born sinful, savage beasts hell-bent on glorifying the flesh and being edified in sin. Ephesians 2:2 refers to those who are not in Christ as "sons of disobedience." Ephesians 2:3 goes on to establish this by saying that we are all "by nature children of wrath." God, who is love, doesn't direct His wrath toward the innocent. Our sinful condition originated in the sin of Adam not because God made us that way. Without receiving Christ and understanding the truth, we spread our condition to our children, and we become enablers to sin and rebellion instead of champions of holiness and chastity. There are two aspects of our problem I want to mention are: the product and the enabler.

We are the product of sin. We were born into sin. It was not something we had to be taught. It was something that already existed within us. Our parents did not have to teach us how to lie, how to kill, how to cheat, how to steal. Sin was ingrained in us from conception. It was ingrained into our very nature. Take a moment to read Psalm 51:5.

The apple is evidence that an apple tree exists. The apple is the product of a matured seed. The seed underwent rigorous activity to grow into the tree that produced the apple. Nevertheless the apple is born of the seed. Through process and procedure, the fruit is born. The same is true for you. You were born into sin and into a world of sin. The sinful influences around you has created an environment suitable for the seed of sin to mature. Your so-called innocence is no more, and you begin to plan out the evil and wickedness that rests in you. As your heart plans to perform evil acts it employs your body. The sinful heart desires to feed the flesh. As our tendency toward sin matures, it demands the use of your body and makes it an instrument of sin. Your arms, hands, eyes, genitalia, become tools of sin to further the sinful inclinations of the heart. Although sin rests firmly in your heart it must employ the body to do its dirtiest work. As time goes on your life begins to reveal the true condition of your sinful heart. This is the state we live in before our eyes are opened to the truth. Before our encounter with Christ we are products of the sin that resides in our heart. Our pre-Christ existence is marred with rebellion and lawless action.

The second aspect of our problem is something I mentioned earlier. It is that we are enablers. An enabler is an individual who helps someone else persist in self-destructive behavior. The enabler tries to convince the abuser that his or her erratic behavior will not have consequences. No man or woman in his or her right mind would want to be considered an enabler. Nevertheless we are partly responsible for the sin and corruption of those around us. We recognize that sin is birthed in our hearts from conception. We are born into it. From there we become products of sin and our body becomes the instrument used to give life to sin. There is no transgression of the law without first sinfulness being present in the heart. We become enablers by introducing and helping others continue in their sinful, self-destructive behavior. We encourage their sinful acts and allow their acts to mature around us. We grow silent in the sight of wrongdoing and do not give truth a voice. Sadly, we must accept that in many instances we are partly responsible for the maturation of sin in those around us.

As enablers we must ask if our contribution to society is beneficial or damaging. Are we assisting others in the destruction of their soul? Are we encouraging others to be damned through the lawlessness of our own sin? Have we reduced the price of our soul so that it is easier for us to be sold back into slavery?

Our most damaging act as enablers is our silence. When we close our mouth and do not give voice to the truth we allow for lawlessness to abound. The truth must be said no matter the crowd or the result. The truth is the truth and it must never be silenced. If we remain silent and refuse to share the truth we are enabling others to persist in behavior that will have eternal consequences.

The issues of life flow from our heart. This means that we become products of the nature of our heart. As products of the sinful nature we enable others to persist in sin. This is our problem, and yes, we need to change. Identifying the problem is one thing. From here we must clearly identify the solution.

TO WHAT?

The identifiable problem is the sinfulness of the heart. Out of the heart flows all the issues of life. It is the root of the tree and it is given life by the fruit it produces. The change must take place from the heart to the heart. To put in another way, we are looking for a transformation from the sinful heart to one that is governed by holiness and submission. The sinful heart glories in sin. It finds rest in pornography, lying, stealing, adultery, homosexuality, and other acts that disrupt the foundation of purity. It matures in a message of grace and yet denies the requirement of holiness, but there cannot be grace without holiness. The grossest offenses are not put on trial in the sinful heart. Even so, there is no need for a judge or jury in a lawless land. With this said we must recognize that the change that is needed is not a "what" as much as it is a "Who." Jesus must be the change. He must reside in every fiber of your being. He must be the initial thought of your day and last thought before you close your eyes to sleep. Your every breath must be dedicated to Him. Jesus does not just become another part of your life. He must become your life's ultimate desire and the only place you reside.

The change we seek will not come from the White House, Parliament or any other legislative, judicial or executive body. Our hope for true deliverance and salvation must come through Jesus. He is the change we need.

I pray you are so consumed with Him that you are ready to give up your own life to live the life He is given for you to live.

We must recognize that we are products of sin. We are not just carriers of the problem; we are the problem. Recognizing our plight will help us see our part in enabling others to mature in their problems and sinful behavior. We can do everything in our power to help others change their behavior, but we will be unsuccessful in getting to the root of the problem. Convincing others to change their habits does nothing more than switch the fruit. It is merely a surface level change. It is like taking an orange from an orange tree and trying to place it on an apple tree. The misplaced orange gives the illusion that the tree has changed its fruit, but soon enough the orange will die away and an apple, the rightful fruit of the tree, will grow in its place. The orange may last for a season, but it will not last forever. The same is true for our actions. If the focus of change is to provide you methods on how to stay out of the bed with someone, how to stop watching pornography and how to stop committing adultery then we have only touched a piece of the puzzle. Switching the fruit does not change the root.

I can train a lion to act like a horse. I can make him jump through hoops. I can make him kneel, gallop, roll over and roar on command. If I put him in a cage and took out his meat he would starve to death. If I put hay in his cage he would continue to starve. You would think that his new actions would produce a new heart, but that is not how it works. The lion is still a raging beast focused on destruction. His entire anatomy is made to fit his dominant, carnivorous nature. The lion does not change just because his actions change. He is still capable of inflicting a lot of pain and damage. The lion does not become a docile animal until his heart is changed. Man can change the actions of the beast; only Christ can change the heart and nature of the beast. Knowing this, we must center our focus on Christ, not good works. Does this mean good works are not important? Absolutely not! The good works we do will come, but as a result of a changed heart. Your actions are evidence to the nature and condition of the heart. I am never surprised when I hear a news story about a bear or a lion attacking a human who is trying to keep them encaged. The cage only serves as a tool of temporary enslavement. Once it is removed or destroyed the beast can roam and kill at will.

Our problem is the sin that resides in our heart. It is not something we could have controlled. We were born with it and are shaped by it. We become products and enablers of it. We place stumbling blocks in the way of other believers and refuse to encourage others to good works. We deny the responsibility to evangelize the lost and give as God commands. Again I say: the change we need is not found in man's ideas or theories. The change we need is not a "what" but a "Who." The change is not a thing or a theory. The change is Jesus Christ. It is through Him that we are changed and born anew. If we fail to understand this we will lower our price tag and sell ourselves to any bidder.

Selling Sex

How much does sex cost where you live? I recognize that this may not be a typical question you are asked every day. You may think that you have to ask a prostitute to get a gauge of the cost of sex; however that is not the case. The sex is free and yet very costly. Allow me a chance to explain this paradox.

Sexually charged content is being piped into your home through the television, radio, computer and cell phones. No matter the method involved, lust is liable and capable of finding a way to get to you. It is free for all who desire it. Pornography is a billion dollar business that captures the lives of children and adults. Its reach goes beyond social and economic status. It does not just affect men, the rich or the curious. It is deadly and its influence is damning.

Advertisements are filled with sex. The images are not subtle any longer. The message is blatant and classless. It is becoming such a part of society that everyone thinks it is normal. While in New York I walked into a clothing store. As I walked in, there stood a model with a skimpy bathing suit on. The message she was sending was clearly one of seduction and sexuality. She was the advertisement for the store, and when I walked in I noticed that she did a good job of bringing in the customers. The store was brimming with young men who were filled with raging hormones. Once they were in the store they were buying the product that would ultimately help the store's profit margin. The model was used as a symbol and an advertisement because of her sex appeal. Her purpose was to attract the attention of all potential customers. She was not selling a bikini; she was selling the idea of sex. And yes, I left the store immediately.

Many times we like to think selling sex only exists with prostitutes. But, that is not always the case. The prostitute is the product of sexual advertisement. She or he becomes the standard in the sex bartering system. The customer gives money or drugs in exchange for use and enjoyment of the other person's body. The prostitute is not seen as a person; she or he is only a means to achieve some selfish and base fulfillment. After the prostitute is used she or he is thrown back out to make yet another deal. You may read this and think that it sounds disgusting. How could someone give or barter himself or herself away like that? Ironically you could be doing the very same thing and not even realize it.

In order to explain this I need to first get you to understand the concept of bartering. To barter is to exchange goods and services without the use of money. It is actually a system we use daily. Prostitution, which is the world's oldest profession, is usually the exchange of sex for money. However the exchange can be for something other than money. Both parties could exchange favors, drugs, alcohol, or a car. The types of exchanges possible are literally limitless. Why is this important for you to know? When we choose to have sex with someone we are involving ourselves in a barter system. You may not exchange sex for money like some, but you are exchanging something. You choose to trade your feelings in exchange for sexual services. You choose to give up your heart to someone in exchange for sex, and sadly we may not think anything is wrong with it.

How about those are still virgins, Cornelius? If you are a virgin, I applaud you. In our day the value of virginity has been cheapened. Most of those who consider themselves to be virgins are not, in the strictest sense of the word. They think that purity of the body is all that is required for virginity. Jesus tells us that adultery begins in the heart. If we choose to look at someone with lust in our heart we are just as guilty as those who have committed the act (Matthew 5:27-28). The act is not done after we have gotten into bed with the person. It is done long before, when we sit and contemplate it in our mind. Purity of the body is ultimately the result of purity of the heart. If the heart is not pure the body is sure to follow. The selling of sex affects the heart. Ironically the selling of sex uses the body in order to reach the heart. Then it is the heart that affects the entire body. Sexual advertisements put the body on display. Sexuality and lust sells at a high premium in order to convince the buyer that the sex on display is worth buying.

The body is a gift from God. Its primary purpose was not to satisfy our carnal desires. Our bodies are to be used to give glory and honor to God. But, because of sin and our failure to obey God's instruction we see women and men being used as sex toys. Their value is reduced to a play thing rather than a child of God. Both men and women are sexually objectified in order to appeal to another person's sexual appetite. Nowadays the appeal has to be broader so no one is left out. The heterosexual, bisexual and homosexual are all catered to by these methods of selling sex. The objectification of both the man and women has helped to create a very superficial society. The advertisements used by marketing companies has created new and distorted standards of beauty. The images used in the sexualized advertisements are edited to give a more sophisticated view of sexuality. However, unsuspecting children do not realize what they are seeing is not real. These easily influenced minds begin to compare their young and still changing bodies to what is being advertised.

You may be one of the many people in our world who

thinks objectifying men and women is not such a bad idea. I would ask that you rethink your stance on the matter. The objectification process transforms men and women into things, and things do not have feelings or desires. Objectification completely erases the desires, opinions, preferences or wants of the woman or man. They are merely motionless things. To be used and discarded without any consideration at all. I would go as far as saying that objectification is worse than slavery. The slave, although held in bondage, has desires, opinions, feelings, wants and preferences. The problem is that the slave cannot express them because he is held in bondage. Objects, unlike slaves, are things that are void of personality. If someone desires to have them, they can be had.

I have spoken some about being sexy and being sexual. Before closing, I believe it is wise to note that being sexy and being sexual are related but different concepts. Being sexy is to inspire sexual feelings in other people. Being sexual is to experience sexual feelings. By this standard, women are referred to as sexy in order to make a sexual appeal to men. The objectification of the woman goes hand-in-hand with society's emphasis of teaching men misplaced priority of pursing women. The central image used of women in advertising is one of being thin and submissive. Men are portrayed as strong and powerful. Our society has changed throughout the years to include a stronger portrait of women to match the strength they are told to exude in society. The "weak woman," who is inaccurately known as the "submissive woman," is shown mostly to carter to the man's dominance and prideful ego. Man's ego notices the submissiveness of women in the advertisement and they are drawn to it. This cultural portrayal of dominance, submission, power, thinness and a host of other attributes helps to push the idea that the body is worth selling.

Sex is a lucrative selling tool in our world today. We are a Rated-R and "XXX" society. It is in our music, our television shows, our schools, our hospitals and even in our churches. Please know that the body is never to be used as a commodity to get something from someone. The body is not a bartering method. It should not be traded for selfish pleasure. It is, and will always be, the temple of our God. It must not be tainted by fornication or any other sexual immorality. We must guard it as any priest would oversee and protect the holy temple.

Slavery

Nathaniel was locked in chains and thrown into a dungeon. There he sat for years contemplating his sentence. Each day he screamed out for help but no one came to his rescue. He could hear the moans and groans of those around him. The prison was filled with men, women, boys and girls who were also being held captive. After years of wanting to be set free, Nathaniel heard a sound in the distance. The noise sounded like the rattling of keys. Nathaniel rushed to the jail door and began to scream out for the one bearing the keys to come let him out of his cell. You see, Nathaniel did nothing to be imprisoned. He was born into the bondage. Nathaniel could hear the sound of the keys as they were brought closer and closer and closer. After years of bondage and torture Nathaniel finally had hope. He hoped this was not another attempt to deceive him. So many times before he had been given false hope. He fully expected to be delivered through different acts, but he was still confined. While the acts of masturbation, fornication, lying, cheating, stealing and other sinful pleasures gave momentary relief, they failed to fully release him from the cell.

After what seemed like an eternity a man appeared before

Nathaniel's cell door. He was not dressed like a guard and he did not act like one either. His countenance was so peaceful and welcoming. He told Nathaniel to step away from the jail door and believe in him. Without hesitation, Nathaniel believed in him. The man grabbed the keys and opened the door that held Nathaniel in bondage for so long. The jail door swung open, the chains fell off and Nathaniel walked out of the cell. "I'm free!" shouted Nathaniel. In between Nathaniel's excitement the man said to him, "Son, you must spend your days telling others about me." As Nathaniel exited the prison he could hear the moans and groans of others who were locked in bondage. He was nearly to the doors ready to escape the prison and never return again, but he soon discovered how difficult it was to truly leave. Nathaniel could not get the words the man had spoken to him out of his head. He could not erase the memory of the torture he had endured while locked in the cell. He could not forget the agony he felt while being thrown in the cell to rot away. He knew he had to turn back to help others who were still in bondage.

Nathaniel rushed back into the prison telling the other prisoners about the man who has the keys to their freedom. They could see that Nathaniel was set free, but that did not help some of them to believe. Only a few would actually believe in the man who was there to set them free. And of those who did believe, only a few turned back to tell others about their newfound freedom. Nathaniel knew the dangers he faced by going back into the prison, but he knew he had to return. He could not live knowing others were suffering and he knew the way of escape.

Nathaniel ran into many problems each time he went back to tell the others about the man who was there to set them free. The primary obstacle Nathaniel faced was this: even though they were bound and restricted, many of the people did not understand their true situation. They were slaves. Those that were trapped in their cells simply would not believe what Nathaniel was telling them. So, they resisted. They doubted and denied what Nathaniel said. He just could not understand why the slaves challenged his efforts.

Is that not the plight of our world today? We live under the false idea of freedom. The freedom of our day means living and doing as we please. It is about living your life how you want it without giving attention to what is right or lawful. Many do not realize it, but freedom is its own form of bondage. A concept of freedom known as hedonism gives the idea that you can do as you desire. You can drink it, smoke it, have sex with it, party with it, dance with it, and eat it without any consequences. The "it" in the equation is left up to the user. If the "it" is a drug then their idea of freedom allows them to entertain it without thinking of the repercussions of their actions. Once people get ahold of this false idea of freedom they become slaves to it. They become slaves to whatever they perceive as right. They live with a false notion that they are free when in actuality they are in bondage to their own lawless way of thinking.

The greatest issue the slave faces is when the truth of the situation is not fully grasped and understood. Namely, that they are a slave. We are all slaves to something and in some way, fashion or form. In Romans 6:16 it reads: *"Do you not know that when you present yourselves to someone as slaves for obedience, you are slaves of the one whom you obey, either of sin resulting in death, or of obedience resulting in righteousness?"* Do you realize this? You are a slave to whatever you submit yourself. Slavery, in itself, is not a bad thing. It becomes bad when your "lord" is bad. For example, if your "lord" is pornography then you are a rebellious, perverse slave. If your Lord is Christ then your slavery is righteous. He adopts you as His own and you become a son. His yoke is easy; however the yoke of perverse slaves is hard. It weighs you down and brings humiliation and death. We tend to associate slavery with a very negative connotation. We attach to it all the atrocities committed in its name. The slavery I am writing about is more so negative than it is positive.

I have had the wonderful opportunity of living and visiting many different places. In some cultures I would assume some tasks are those performed by slaves. I am speaking more in psychological terms more than the physical. I have met people who were slaves to food. They sold themselves for fast foods and unhealthy desserts. The food owned them. They would do whatever they had to do to answer to their master. Sadly, the food was and is killing them. I am not talking about healthy foods either. I am talking about foods that are drenched in grease, loaded with sugar and caked with salt. I know those foods. I used to eat them. I was once a slave to them. I would hide oatmeal raisin cookies under my bed, try to sneak and eat Whoopers without my wife finding out and I felt like I had to have an eighteen-ounce steak. I would not go as far as saying the steak was bad. It was just that it was too much, and I would load it down with butter and salty sauces. I did what most people do today. I took something that could have been somewhat healthy and I loaded it down with all these additives. You may be thinking that our world's addiction with food is not such a bad thing. I would ask you to reconsider. Slavery to food does not have just one master. First you are a slave to food. Then you are a slave to pharmaceutical drugs. The unhealthy foods destroy your body; then you need the medicine to keep you alive. The goal of a company is to increase their profit margin. The same is true for pharmaceutical companies. They want to increase their profits. If you get healthy, you no longer need their medication; thus their profits fall. Do not think slavery to food is a light thing.

Ultimately slavery in any form is dangerous and restrictive. It is a very important issue that cannot be ignored.

It is found throughout Scripture. What is also throughout Scripture is God releasing the enslaved from their bondage. After being released the majority begin to live as if slavery did not exist. They turn on the One who released them and live as if nothing has changed. In fact nothing much has changed. We are still enslaved. What is important is awareness. We must be made aware of our slavery. I feel as if this is one of the greatest components of salvation. If we are not aware of our slavery to sin we will never realize that we need to be released. If we do not realize our plight to sin we will never realize that we need the Savior. The man who thinks he is free does not realize he is enslaved. He must first be made aware of his slavery, and honestly, that was my goal in writing this chapter. I want to make you aware of your slavery.

Consider Nathaniel again. He was locked in the cell. The sound of keys gave him hope. That simple sound sparked something inside him and brought great joy and excitement. The keys represented an opportunity for him to be released from his bondage. There are couple of thoughts I would ask you to consider: Do you know you are enslaved? If so, have you been told about the Man who has the keys to your freedom? I pray each time you hear the Gospel preached it sounds like the rattling of keys. Do not do like some have and rush out of the prison without considering those who are still left behind, locked inside. Slavery still exists so we must make others aware of it.

Resistance

The slave must obey his master because he belongs to him. We are either slaves to sin or slaves to Christ. Our allegiance is to the master we are enslaved to serve. When sin is our master, we are incapable of truly resisting it. Most often we employ willpower to assist us in staying away from sin. There is one big problem with willpower: "will" has no "power." Willpower, alone, cannot stop the bondage of sin. There is only one way to stop sin's bondage, and He is Jesus Christ. We must repent of our sins. Christ is faithful and just to forgive us. After we have come to Christ, we are empowered by the Holy Spirit. We are able to resist sin's dominance by His power; thereby transferring our allegiance and becoming slaves to righteousness.

Those who are born of God belong to Him. Christ followers should desire to do all that pleases Him. They will obey Him and refrain from involving themselves in anything that displeases Him. They recognize that God hates sin, so they despise it as well. They take a stand with God, not against Him. They do not live in habitual sin. They are free from the slavery of sin because of Jesus and they are no longer under the penalty of death. I pray you understand the work that God is trying to accomplish in you. If needed, reread it until it gets in your heart.

We have dealt with the remedy to sin over and over again already. Now I want to focus on the actions we take after we have been joined in union with Christ by faith. I want to focus on our resistance of sin.

Many do not understand the importance of resisting sin. Hebrews 12:4 reads *"Ye have not yet resisted to blood, striving against sin."* Based on this verse let me ask you a question. Have you resisted sin to such a point that you began to sweat blood? I would wager that for most, if not all, of us would be a resounding "no." We like to say that we are resisting sin, but that is not always the truth. I hear people say that they are constantly fighting the good fight against sin. Most of the time that is a lie. They are not fighting; they are submitting to sin. Fighting involves resisting. It involves being on guard just in case the enemy goes on the attack. Fighting is as much about the defense as it is the offense. Fighting does not include laying the sword down and lowering the shield. It is about making sure the whole armor of God is in place to resist any attack that might be launched against us.

The armor of God is designed to help us fight our sin and the influence of in. When we walk out the door and we are not prepared to face the day we put our lives in danger. The shield blocks the blows that will come, but it also shelters the soldier. The sword is an offensive weapon that helps us to combat the assault of the enemy. If both are down the soldier is prey for the predator of our souls. One major component of the soldier's armor is the belt. The belt must be on and it must be tight. If it is not, the entire suit will be off. The belt also holds the sword. If the belt is sagging the sword sags and the whole outfit sags. Our "pants" are then really on the ground—spiritually speaking. The armor is heavy, and the belt is needed. The truth of the matter is we cannot afford to sag any longer.

Resisting sin is a daily reality and conscious decision. Resisting the temptations that come is not something we do by accident. We must be cautious of what we watch, read, and listen to. We must think on what is pure, holy and excellent. When someone offers you a night of sin, resist it. It is okay to turn down any offer that requires you to disobey God. You do not have to go out to the nightclubs, get drunk, get high or get in the bed with someone other than your spouse. You do not have to look at pornography or listen to lustful music just because your feelings tell you to do so. Through Christ, you can resist it.

One practical application is to remember one of the greatest tools God gives to us in relation to resisting sin. God has given us to ability to pray. When temptation knocks at the door of your heart, pray to God. Ask Him to strengthen you above the temptation's ability to influence you. Ask Him to heal you of the pain of your past and the issues you still deep down inside.

A second practical activity to consider is singing. I know you might be asking yourself, "What in the world is Cornelius talking about?", but I want you to hear me out. I found it very difficult to watch pornography while I was signing "Amazing Grace." The words would touch my heart and remind me of my allegiance to Christ. As soon as the temptation would come I would begin to sing. It helped me to stay away from sin and approaching temptations and I am sure it will help you as well.

A third possibility is to run. I know that sounds too simple, but you know everything that is simple is not always something we do. When you are put in a position where you are tempted, run! You do not just end up in someone's bed. Most of the time you have planned the act long before it is completed. Instead of laying down, get up and run.

One final practical tip is to stay surrounded and accountable to others. We usually do not commit sin when people are around. Our society is becoming bolder with their relation to sin; however that does not mean we have to do so. It is important to assemble with other believers. Get around them so they are able to assist you in your journey. Call your friends, brothers, sisters and elders on the phone late at night when you are tempted. Tell them what is going on with you. Tell them that you are in a situation where your witness could be destroyed because of the temptation knocking on the door of your heart. Keep yourself surrounded.

"Be subject therefore unto God; but resist the devil, and he will flee from you. Draw nigh to God, and he will draw nigh to you. Cleanse your hands, ye sinners; and purify your hearts, ye doubleminded. Be afflicted, and mourn, and weep: let your laughter be turned to mourning, and your joy to heaviness. Humble yourselves in the sight of the Lord, and he shall exalt you." James 4:7-10

Not For Sale

Samuel was a good servant. He always did what was asked of him without complaining. He was known for his hard work, dedication and attention to detail. His father trained him up well. He took great pride in his work and he did not allow anything or anyone to stand in his way.

Samuel's master was known for being very direct and particularly focused. He would set his crosshairs on a goal, and he would not abandon it for any reason. He would remain committed to the task until it was complete. Samuel and his master made a great team.

Samuel was not always a servant of his master. He was known all over the town for his carpentry. He could make just about anything. He was very skilled at what he did. One day the master was walking alone through the town. He spotted Samuel hard at work on what he thought was one of his best creations—a handcrafted stool. The master walked into Samuel's shop and said to him, "Son, leave what you are doing behind. Come follow me." Samuel believed in the master immediately upon hearing his voice. He dropped his tools where he stood and he followed him. Samuel did not turn back to see what he left behind. He just left. He did not consult with the other carpenters or call his family to ask for their opinion. He believed in the master's call and he obeyed him without hesitation.

Samuel did not just leave behind his carpentry business. He left his entire life and comfortable way of living. He left everything that was familiar to him just so he could become a servant to the master. His friends and family did not understand it. They continued to question him about his decision, but Samuel was determined to remain obedient to the master. His father's death did not detour him. He did not turn back. He did not go back to his home to deliver the news to his family. He did not take his hand from the plow. He just kept going.

The master was very wise. While out with Samuel one day the master noticed one of the richest men in the town—Isaac. Isaac was known for his wealth. He wore the finest linens and always had the best foods. Crowds followed him just so they could rummage through his leftovers. He was not a charitable man. He was often rude and haughty. The master saw Isaac standing next to some of the countrymen. As the master walked up to Isaac the men began to back away. Isaac turned around to see what caused the men to step back and there stood the master. "Isaac, follow me," said the master. Isaac, looking confused and frustrated that the master would interrupt him, looked to the master saying, "I don't need to follow you. I have everything I've always wanted. I have more riches than the kings of the East. My chariots outnumber the armies of the West. I have more handmaidens and servants than any man I know. I reap where I do not sow and give as I please. I have amassed this wealth on my own, and I don't need you. In fact why would I, a wealthy master, choose to divest my wealth and all that I have just so I could follow you? Look at your lowly servant Samuel. He's given his life to you. He lives to serve you. What a loss! He's pathetic and so are you!"

The master stared straight into Isaac's eyes. "Isaac, let it be recorded that you denied to follow after me. Your wealth is your god. You've grown comfortable in your way of living. Let it be known that your kingdom will be destroyed. The moths will eat up what you have stored, your servants will make you their slave and all that you have reaped will return to nothing." Isaac looked confused at the master's words, but he was undeterred. He grabbed his slaves, mounted his donkey and rode back to his palace.

Samuel and the master continued walking. As they walked, the master would stop to teach Samuel. He would demonstrate the principle of sowing and reaping by planting seeds in the ground and waiting for the harvest. He taught as they lived life together. He made every opportunity an opportunity to learn and grow together.

As years passed the number of servants grew. Many men chose to give up their way of living to follow the master. The master asked the servants to turn and follow him as they travelled back into the city to teach. As they were walking they noticed a man sitting in a dark corner. The master walked over to him. His clothes were very dirty, his hair was disheveled and his countenance had fallen. The master looked down at the man saying, "Isaac, stand to your feet." Samuel and the other servants were amazed at what they saw. Samuel walked towards Isaac and said, "What happened to you?" Isaac said, "The moths ate all of my fine linens, my servants made me their slave and my kingdom was destroyed. I lost all I had. Please ask your master to consider allowing me to follow him. I beg of you." The master, a very forgiving man, asked Isaac to follow him yet again. This time Isaac agreed. From that day forward Isaac was one of the greatest servants the master would have besides Samuel. Samuel and Isaac would forge a friendship that could not be broken.

As years passed the number of servants continued to grow. Some who began to follow early began to fall away. Some died along the journey. Some just gave up trying and returned to their old way of living. The master was becoming a nuisance to the ruler of the city. He wanted the master and the servants to be removed for good. Late one evening the guards took the master captive. They beat and tortured him for days. On the seventh day the ruler had the master killed. The news of his death quickly spread throughout the city. Samuel, Isaac and the rest of the servants knew they would be next. They decided to travel outside the city to teach all they had learned from the master.

While trying to leave Samuel was captured and sent to the ruler. "I've heard great things about you," the ruler said to Samuel. "I've heard how hard working and confident you are. I've heard of all the good things you have done. I'm impressed. As you already know I had your master put to death. Samuel, you followed him for nothing. He paid you nothing. I want to make you an offer! Come be my servant and all the riches of the world will be yours. You will drink from the finest glasses, eat the best foods, wear the finest clothes and eat from the ruler's table. All that your feet touch will be at your command. I can give all of this to you. This is the price I'm willing to pay. Now what do you say?" The guards unshackled Samuel from his chains and threw him before the ruler's feet. Samuel lowered his head before the ruler and said, "Sir, your offering is too kind. It is more than I have ever had in my life. To have the opportunity to live like a king is more than I ever would have thought possible, but I must decline your offer. See, the master taught me all I know. His words pierced my heart and convicted me to change. His life was a testimony of true wealth. He gave his time to helping others who were in need. He did not have to pay me with worldly possessions because his life and his teachings secured my eternity destiny. My payment may seem low as I bow before you, but it will be great in eternity. Your offer is filled with worldly vices that will soon die away. Your kingdom will not last forever, the locusts will eat your fine clothes, your table will fall, your food will spoil and your death will be gruesome. Although your offer sounds good I must inform you that I am one with the master. Sir, I am not for sale!"

After that encounter with the ruler, Samuel was put to death along with the other servants. The only one to escape was Isaac. He traveled the world sharing all that the master taught him. He would not compromise. He remained faithful to what was true and excellent. He, too, recognized he was not for sale. Are you?

The Sales Plan

A good sales plan gives direction and expectation for the team to perform. Those who are tasked to make the sale are told to go by the plan that is presented to them. The sales plan includes the target audience, the incentive for making the sales and identifies the training and marketing support that will help the team achieve their objectives. I want you to pay attention to what we will discuss in the next few pages. Make sure you are in a place where you can focus on what you are about to read. I do not want you to be distracted.

We have read a great deal about the importance of Christ. He is our only hope; the right answer; the only identifiable solution to escaping the bondage of sin and death. To properly convey this point I want to break down for you the sales plan of our redemption and potential damnation. I will cover each part of the plan; then finish by explaining why it is important for you to know the plan.

First, we must cover the objective of the sales plan. The plan is in place so the team is able to increase revenue by either winning new customers or using their existing customers to expand the business. Who or what is the team? In this equation the team consists of Satan and his legion of demons. Their sales strategy is founded on deception. Their target audience consists of me, you and every other person who has been born of a woman. Like any sales plan, the plan must be centered on growth and each member of the team is given a responsibility. Since the ultimate goal is to increase the revenue of the company by either winning new customers or working with existing ones, the team must know their target audience. They must know how to communicate with the audience in a way to encourage them to buy-in to the plan.

THE TARGET AUDIENCE

Before discussing the buy-in I want to spend some time going over the target audience, you and me. We have been adopted as children of God. We are given an opportunity to be born-again through and by Jesus Christ. Satan hates the true Christ follower. Satan hates whomever God loves, and God loves us. As adopted, born-again children we become part of the family. We begin to resemble the household where we now make our residence. Seeing that we are born of God's seed, our actions begin to embody more of the Father's character. We bear a resemblance of the Father and carry the same standard as the other family members in our household of faith.

Satan is still jealous of our relationship with God. His

ancient hatred still runs deep. He hates us because of our resemblance to the Father. Satan takes no concern for those he has won over. The deceived, the fallen and the bound are all under his yolk; therefore he takes no thought of them. He spends his time sending the sales force after those who pose an ongoing threat to his kingdom in hopes that they will buy the committed back to him.

The target audience is not those who proclaim themselves as Christians. It is not those who act as if God is their father. It does, however, consist of those who are truly reborn of God. They show fruit of their change. Their lives prove they are children of God. Their private actions match their public performance. If they stumble, they do not stay down long. They do not pursue sin; they pursue God. They seek the kingdom of God first, carry their cross, deny themselves and follow without hesitation. They are true to their word, and they will not break their allegiance to follow anyone else even if it means they will have to die for their convictions. The target audience is a major threat to Satan's government. To him, they must be destroyed. If these holy rebels are not destroyed they could cause serious damage in the rebellious world we live in today.

One of our many assignments as believers is to pray because praying is a serious threat to Satan and his sales plan. The communication we have with God is more than what he can handle. He is estranged. He cannot get back into the household; therefore he would like nothing more than to destroy those who are in the household. Since he cannot touch God, he goes after His children. And when he goes after them, he unleashes every weapon available to him. The book of Job is a great book to reference this point. I recommend you make some time to sit down to read it.

As the target audience we recognize that we have a great responsibility to share the truth with others so more souls may be won to Christ. Our hope is that God opens the blinded eyes of those who cannot see and opens the ears of those who are deaf. With this responsibility we must preach both with our words and with our actions. Our sermons must be born out of conviction and the truth should be laced with passion. We know that it is important to share the Gospel. How else will people know unless they hear? How will people hear unless there is a preacher? We preach fully expecting God to convict the hearer to repentance. We hope for liberation; therefore we go into the entire world carrying the truth and making disciples.

Our task sounds like an easy one, but the execution is somehow lost in the maze of worldly comfort. Mindless activities and a lot of busy work sidetrack us. We lose focus of the objective; thereby giving the enemy an opportunity to do what we have been tasked to do—recruit more for the team.

Make no mistake about it. Satan and his sales force are at work recruiting more and more people to his team through deception. He has widened the way to destruction in order to fit more along the path. He knows the target audience well. He has dealt with us for centuries. His deception did not start the day your eyes were opened to the truth. He started back with a woman named Eve and her husband, Adam.

THE BUY-IN

Satan convinced Eve and Adam to buy-in to his sales pitch. I must admit that it was very convincing. In Genesis 2 God clearly gives Adam a command telling him he can eat of every tree of the garden except the tree of the knowledge of good and evil. After God created Eve, she and Adam were together. Satan appeared before them to try and convince them what God said was not true. He twisted the truth in order to appeal to their emotions. I am sure Eve knew she should not eat of the tree of knowledge. In fact, I know for sure that Adam knew. Satan wanted to convince Eve she was missing out on something by not being able to decipher the difference between good and evil just as God could. The fruit became appealing. Soon enough, Eve ate the fruit and handed it over to Adam. Satan was successful in causing Adam and Eve to disobey God. He got them to buy-in to his plan. The root of his plan was deception. Ultimately, he got

Adam and Eve to rethink the command God gave them. He caused them to doubt. He fed them a huge lie laced with a little truth in order to appeal to their emotions, causing them to rethink what they heard.

Satan's tactics are ancient, but he is still using them to maximum effect today. He is still deceiving people to this day. His sales plan is still in the works. He offers a lie wrapped in a little bit of truth. It is like me giving you a gift. The gift is nicely wrapped in the best wrapping paper created. You marvel at how nice it looks. It appeals to your emotions. All you can think about is what is inside. You wonder if what is inside is as wonderful as what you see on the outside. You carefully unwrap the wrapping paper to see that inside the box is a bunch of stinky trash. Most of the contents inside the box are moldy and it smells horrible. After looking inside you realize you were fooled. You thought the contents inside would match what you saw on the outside. Unfortunately, you were greatly deceived.

Consider all the things you have ever known about life. Consider all the sources you have learned from concerning the way you live. Are those sources credible? Were you fed a big lie wrapped in a little truth? Is your life only a product of a message that catered to your emotions? Are you like Eve in the sense that you wanted the fruit because it looked appealing to you? You see the sex looks appealing but the STD's you contracted afterward are not. Telling a lie seems appealing, but being found out as a liar is not. A little idolatry seems like it will not be so bad until it convinces you to lose focus and turn your back on God. I am not making this stuff up. Look at Israel's history. Their relationship with God was back-and-forth. They would not let go of the idols even when God continued to rescue them from their difficulties. They continued to murmur, complain, doubt and turn their back on God.

Have you been convinced to buy-in to Satan's plans? Are you like those who live with this motto: I'm going to live my life the way I want to live it? If so, please know that it is a dangerous way to live. You did not create yourself; therefore you cannot dictate the direction of your life. I am a firm believer in the concept of freewill, but I do not believe that freewill overrides our responsibility to God. Although I am free to choose my own way I do not turn my back on God. Yes, it is a choice, but, with God, I settle the choice by aligning myself with Him and Him only. I cannot claim Him and Satan. I cannot be on both teams. If "CHRISTIAN" is written across my jersey, I must get in the game. There can be no idle players.

Do not buy-in to the schemes of the enemy. He will cater to your emotions, feed your doubts, starve your faith, introduce deception and try to convince you that the consequences for your actions will either be delayed or turn out to be nonexistent.

Please understand that just because the consequences do not come right way does not mean they will not eventually come. Today's society is ready and bold in its efforts to discount the return of Jesus because they say that they do not see His return happening. They think His delay is a sign that He is not coming. They mock Him as if He is not real and do all they can to undermine the credibility of His followers. They perform acts of evil and mock God when the consequences are not immediate. Their hearts are unrepentant. Those who claim to be believers but are not will soon enough turn away from the faith. They begin to follow those who mock the Gospel. They believe the lies, and they return to their old way of living.

Please know that Satan's plan is not just in the streets. It has made its way into our homes. It comes through our computers, our radios and our televisions. It is in our schools, our hospitals, and our government. It is in the White House, and yes, it is in the temple. Wolves in sheep's clothing are sent out to deceive and distract. They scatter the sheep instead of leading them. They lure weak-minded women and men with their smooth words of deception. Wolves travel in packs. They surround the prey before attacking. They prefer to attack at night or in an area where the prey cannot see them when they come. The same is true for the wolves in the pulpit today. They scatter the sheep with their deceptive talk. They solicit money from weak-willed people. People who give their money hoping for some promised spiritual blessing. They portray God as a "genie-in-a-bottle" ready to grant their every request.

At the heart of their deception is this: they turn grace into lasciviousness. They have made it out to be something perverse. They present God's grace as more of a reason to continue sinning instead of the reason to abstain from sin. They turn love into a selfish, human desire. Very few preach righteous love. Our love for God is based on the truth that He first loved us. It is because of Him that we are capable of loving. Our love is demonstrated by following His commands, not ignoring them as if they did not exist. If our love for God is true then we will vindicate it by being obedient to His commands. What are His commands? We are to love God and love others as we love ourselves. We should never deviate from these commands. Jesus said that all of the teaching found in the law and of the prophets hang on these two commands (Matthew 22:40).

Remember that the objective for the team is to increase profits by winning new customers or expanding the operation with existing customers. Satan already has his existing customers covered. Our job is to share the light of the Gospel in dark places. We are called to go out amongst the wolves, not run from them. We have not been given a spirit of fear. We do not run from the opposition. We stand ready to withstand the assault knowing that our service will bring a righteous reward. Satan's plan to win new customers is in full effect. His prime objective is accomplished through deception. I am sure his quotas are high. Make sure you are not one of them. Don't buy-in to his plan!

THE TERRITORY

An effective sales plan identifies a particular territory to target for growth. The target can be either numerical or geographical. The plan allocates certain territories to different representatives. The enemy's territory is limited to this world. His range is controlled. It does not supersede the sovereignty of God. The enemy roams like a roaring lion. His bite is ineffective and his roar is hollow.

THE PRODUCT

An effective sales plan also identifies the product it will sell to the customer. In this equation the product being sold is a lie. The origin of the lie is from the ultimate liar, Satan. Those who choose to believe it begin to live the lie. They take on the very nature of worldly deception until it corrupts their heart. The enemy knows he does not have to give many lies. He just needs to get you, me and everyone else to fully believe one lie. After the first lie is believed, the customer is liable to continue buying into the plan.

Lies are convincing. They target our curiosity and distort our awareness. The enemy knows he must market the lie in such a way that it appeals to our carnal, sensual nature. He makes it alluring. He dangles it like bait before the person until she or he takes it. Since our environment is conducive and fertile for growing more lies, the enemy knows that once the customer has tasted one lie she or he will come back for more. As believers we should not attempt to taste the lies. We must not go after them. Instead, we taste and see that the Lord is good. Once we have tasted the goodness of the Lord we will never want to go back. We will hunger and thirst after righteousness. We will yearn to have Christ as our daily bread. We will thirst after Him as our living water. He becomes our heart's desire.

MARKETING PLAN

It is ineffective to have a product and not have a plan to market it. The product must be marketed appropriately so that it fully caters to customer. As I have stated before, the marketing plan is filled with sensuality, carnality and deception. Look out at our society today. Our television shows, music and billboards are filled with lustful images that appeal to our basest desires and feed our carnal nature. The pictures are alluring and the seduction is real. The marketing plan is designed to get you to consider the product. The question you must ask yourself is this: is the plan working on you?

Breaking Point

There comes a point in everyone's life when they realize life is more than just finding pleasure out of momentary opportunities and sinful indulgences. I will never forget when that happened for me. I was 22-years-old, living alone, with no real understanding what it means to have true freedom. I was still in bondage to all kinds of sin. I wanted to hide it, but it would continue to spill over into other areas of my life. I had just finished "rededicating" my life for the thousandth time. I was at that point where I was saying, "This time is going to be different, Lord! I really mean it this time." Although the words came from my lips, they were not true.

My heart was still determined to return to the sin I continued to say I would run against. I did not truly trust that Jesus could or would set me free. I would say my little prayer in hopes God knew my heart. And, in fact, He did know my heart. He knew it was wicked. I realized I could be exposed and the exposure would be devastating. I could end up losing everything, but it did not matter. I was determined to go back to my sin. Like most do today, I tried to use grace as an excuse to continue in sin. I read Titus 2:11-14, and my mind quickly changed. I encourage you to take a break from the book, grab your Bible, look up Titus 2:11-14 and read it over and over again until you get the revelation of what it says. Once you are done you can move on to the next paragraph.

I was the dog that constantly ran back to its vomit. Like so many, I was hungry and thirsty for sin even though I knew what I was doing was wrong. Over the years I have come to terms with this truth: I cannot have it even if I desire it. I can honestly say the desire for sin is not as strong today as it was years ago, but I cannot rightly say the desire is gone. I am tempted often, but I know I cannot give in to sin. I must be strong in faith and resist the temptation. The same is true for you. You must resist the temptation whenever it comes. As you continue to resist it, the desire for it will die away. I know that to be true in my own experience.

You must also be active in your relationship with Christ. He does such a work in us that we are able to deny the ungodliness we once indulged. Through Him, we are able to bury our old sinful ways and be resurrected with Him with a new nature. Then, we must renew our minds. We cannot expect new actions if we are constantly feeding ourselves tainted, perverse information. We can only give out what we put in. If we put trash in, we can expect trash to come out. This is why it is imperative to be diligent in our prayer life and daily study of the

Word of God. It is vital that the way we think matures to match our new nature in Christ.

As we walk in our Christian journey we come to points in our life where we realize that our life is not what it is supposed to be. I remember speaking to a young man who was devastated because of his actions. He called me late one night crying after jumping out of bed with a random woman. He said he met her in a bar that same day, and she agreed to take him back to her apartment so they could have sex. He did not know her. He did not know if she had any sexually transmitted diseases. All he knew was that he wanted to have sex. Oddly enough, this was not his first time doing this. He was distraught because he realized that he was sleeping with a different woman every night for over 7 months. Something happened that night to him that he was not able to explain. All he knew was that he could not get in the bed with the woman. My words to him were simple: "Run!" He called me while in her bathroom, so he pulled up his pants, put on his shirt and ran out of her house. I was on the phone with him for a couple hours as we spoke about the encounter. I was finally able to calm him down and encourage him to seek the Lord in prayer. That night changed his entire life. There was one thing he continued to say over and over again: "Cornelius, I'm at my breaking point." Let's explore and define what he meant.

You have reached your breaking point when you are no longer capable to dealing with a particular situation. It is when a situation is so critical that you begin to shut down and your strength decreases to a point of weakness. This young man experienced his breaking point. The situation he was in had gotten to the point point where he could no longer continue to do what he was doing. He knew that what he was doing was wrong. He could no longer sell himself to the highest bidder, and he refused to be a slave to sin and immorality. He had reached his breaking point point.

When he reached his breaking point he had to make a decision. He had to decide whether he was going to continue doing what he was doing or turn away from his old ways and finally and completely submit to Christ. He could no longer waver between two options. He had to make a decision, and, thankfully, his decision was a righteous one. At the time of writing this book, the young man is still committed in his relationship with the Lord. His sacrifice is admirable and faith is sure. He is at a point where he is able to share his testimony with others in hopes they too will reach their breaking point. That is not everyone's reality though. For some, it takes something that serious for them to wake up to reality. It is sad but true.

My hope and prayer is that you will not have to go that far. My hope is that you will not have something deadly or dangerous happen to you. I hope you will become aware of your need to submit totally to the Lord Jesus.

I know what it is like to have these experiences and still deny Christ. I will never forget when I got into an accident driving down the interstate. I had the car on cruise control. From out of nowhere, it started to rain. I immediately put my foot on the brake and I hydroplaned off the road, tumbling down a hill and hitting a tree. While I was tumbling I cried out to God for help. It was as if time stood still. I could see the CDs spinning around my face and it was like my phone was floating in the air. Once I hit the tree I reached over to grab my phone, which was in pieces. I managed to put it back together piece by piece. Then, I immediately called 911 for assistance. I was shaken up pretty badly, but I was not hurt at all. The radio was still playing and the air conditioner was still going. I looked over to my left and all I could see was the tree I just hit. My driver side door was pressed up on my arm, so I crawled out through the passenger side door.

Once outside, I walked up the hill to meet a bystander. He looked at me and asked, "Do you know if the person in that car is okay?" I told him I was the person in that car. He did not believe me. After looking back at the car I realized why he did not believe me. The car was damaged beyond recognition, but I did not have a scratch or a bruise to show for it. The tree was also damaged. The stranger looked at me and said, "God must really have something in store for you. By the looks of that car, you should be dead." Those words struck me in my heart. The police, fire department and the ambulance finally arrived. After evaluating the situation, the car was towed away and I was driven off to a nearby Waffle House to wait for my family to pick me up. I was still a little shaken. I could still hear the words the bystander said to me. I knew at that moment that I needed to make some changes in my life, but, honestly, I did not. I went right back to my old ways even though I just had a very close encounter with death.

I am sure you have had some breaking points in your life as well. I am also sure, like me, you did not fully decide to submit your life to Christ. You forgot about the experience after the emotionalism faded away. It is like those who always walk down to the altar in a church service because they are caught up in the emotionalism of the moment. They are drawn to the pastor's invitation for salvation because the music is playing softly, the fog machine is going and the cries and sobs of others can be heard throughout the room. They get up to walk down to the front to cry a few tears only to return and go right back to the same sin they supposedly left at the altar. It was just an act—a big emotional production. Do not allow this to describe you. Make the decision today to fully surrender it all to Christ. Lay down your dreams, will, goals and aspirations so He can resurrect you and fill you with His passion, will and desires for your life.

The ironic thing about having a breaking point is that we all need one. I am convinced that it is difficult for a person to honestly receive the Savior if she or he does not think she or he needs saving. A prideful man does not think he needs saving. His salvation is in his own way of thinking and his strength. He is his own savior. The breaking point causes his will and pride to be shattered. He realizes that he cannot do it on his own and that he needs help. He reaches the verge of collapse and realizes he needs help before taking a plunge over the cliff. I love it when I meet men and women who have reached their breaking point. They are the most humble and receptive people.

Have you reached your breaking point? Have you fully ignored the two options placed before you? If so, it is time to make a righteous decision. It is time to fully submit yourself to Christ. I recommend that you get involved in a Word-based church that teaches the convictions of sin, the hope of Christ and the seriousness of eternity. Do not wait another day. Do not put this off any longer. You read these words for a reason. I am sure God is tugging at your heart right now. Go ahead and put the book down. Go to Him in prayer. Pour your heart out to Him. Confess your sins. Confess to Him that you need the

Savior Jesus Christ. Confess that you cannot do it on your own. Let your tears be real. Let you heart truly be broken over your sin and rejoice over the hope we have in Christ. The time is now. It is time to break!

Whose Puppet Are You?

A puppet is someone who can be manipulated or someone whose actions are controlled by others. A puppeteer is someone who manipulates puppets in order to create an illusion of life. The puppeteer serves to pull the strings of the puppet. He speaks for the puppet, controls its every movement and makes it move in any direction he desires. The puppet has strings attached to the head, back and hands to control the arms and strings attached to the knee to control the legs. Throughout this chapter I want you to ask yourself this question: Whose puppet am I?

There are many puppeteers in our day. Technology has created a fantastic way for information to travel quickly around the world. I can easily connect with people around the world at the click of a button. Technology has become a blessing and a curse in many ways. It is a blessing because it allows for truth to travel around the world. However, it can also be a curse because it also allows for false information to do the same. Corrupt and wicked men and women can use social media to promote and champion causes that go against the Word of God. These men and women use sweet and cunning tactics to lure people in, only to devour them with false information. Sadly, many do not really see the deception. They do not see how they are puppets in the hands of wicked puppeteers.

Television has become a great way to promote causes and theories that are not supported by the Word of God. Television does what the name implies; it 'tells a vision'. We must be cautious of the vision it is communicating and the purpose it is championing.

As stated above, puppeteers manipulate puppets in order to create an illusion of life. The radio, books, friends, family and television provide information, which has the potential of being misleading and assists in creating an illusion of life. The puppets live with the illusion that they are truly living, but this false illusion of life is based on broken perspectives and a perverse view of things. Have you created an illusion of life based on the twisted and tainted words of this world? Are you being manipulated or controlled by half-truths, false concepts, bitter family members, hurtful strangers and/or vengeful enemies posing as friends? Are you someone's puppet?

In order to properly use the puppet, the puppeteer must use manipulative tactics to constrain the puppet in his or her web of lies. She or he will use any attempt to control someone else—especially emotional manipulation. The manipulator will use tears, persuasive speech, fear tactics or violence in order to push his or her cause and further entangle the manipulated in his or her web of deceit. Many times the manipulator could use intellectual intimidation, empty threats, belittling, making you think you are in debt or obligated to serve, guilt, shame or make you think what you want is what you need. The manipulator uses his or her influence shrewdly or to achieve an unfair advantage. They may also use fraudulent means to alter or falsify his or own achievements. Many times the puppet does not think she or he is trapped in a dangerous web of manipulation. And there are times when the puppet grows comfortable in the web of lies and deceit. When being manipulated the puppet does not have to think, take a stand on issues, have to be responsible or have to grow or mature.

I believe the media is a great representation of the society. Our programming is filled with lust and anger. Children are exposed to things at a much earlier age. I have had many discussions with young men who have been influenced by video games, music lyrics and television shows. Their entire perception of reality has been altered. They live in a false world that has been created by perversion and for perversion. The liberalism of our day is truly sickening. It brings me to my knees daily. I cannot help but think about my children having to grow up in this perverse world. It is truly frightening.

I have encountered many manipulative men and women

in my day. I was once one of them. I would seek to control others through fear tactics, intellectual intimidation, empty threats and guilt. I have had others who have made me think I was obligated to serve them. They made me think that if I did not serve them I would be damned. This happens a great deal in ministry. I have known pastors to use manipulative tactics to try to restrain congregants to remain in their church or make them continue to serve. Their tactics are so cunning they can easily be mistaken for truth. Many of these men and women twist Scripture to validate their point and further their cause. It is demonic in nature and biblically inaccurate at best. Are you being manipulated right now? Are you involved in a manipulative relationship? Have you been given false information to create an illusion of life?

You may not realize this but much of who you are is based on what you have been taught or what you have learned from those closest to you. You are a sum total of the words you have allowed to define you. Have you bought into the manipulative propaganda of our day? Many are spreading ideas and rumors for the purpose of destroying a cause, a person or an institution. Look at the way our Savior Jesus Christ is being referenced in our day. Movies and shows portray Him as a powerless, fictional character without any standards. It is a sinister tactic. However, many buy into the lies each and every day. The media is a dangerous force, and it has created slaves to its demonic tactics. We must wake up and stop buying into the propaganda.

Satan, the god of this world, is a master manipulator. He twisted the words of God to Adam and Eve in the book of Genesis, and, unfortunately, his tactic was successful. He tried to do the same to Jesus while He was fasting for forty days and forty nights. However, Jesus countered his demonic attacks by speaking the words of the Father. He remained firm and sure in the truth. He did not waiver. We must realize that Jesus Christ has come to cut our strings from the deceitful works of the devil. We have been bought with a price, not by silver and gold but by the precious blood of Christ. We have been ransomed from the bondage of sin. We are no longer under the authority of this world or have to be manipulated by its dangerous tactics. Our puppet strings have been cut loose. We are no longer obligated to speak the deceitful words of the devil. We speak the words of Christ. He changes our heart, plants our feet on solid ground, puts our hands to the plow and assures us of truth that supersedes any lies we obtained through manipulative conversation.

I want to ask you to do something that is very practical. I want you to get out some paper and write out your influencers. Be honest with yourself. If you have been influenced by television, make sure you include it in your list. Be as specific as you can be. Include the exact name of the television show. Write down songs and music genres that have had an influence. List these things so you can see how you have been enchanted by wickedness and perversion. After writing it all down make a decision to cut the strings once and for all. Romans 12:2 reads, "And do not be conformed to this world, but be transformed by the renewing of your mind, so that you may prove what the will of God is, that which is good and acceptable and perfect." James 4:4 reads, "You adulteresses, do you not know that friendship with the world is hostility towards God? Therefore whoever wishes to be a friend of the world makes himself an enemy of God." Do you see the importance of cutting those strings from worldly influence? It is vital. Your eternity depends on it! End the adulteress relationship and untie the strings of the manipulative puppeteer. Do not continue living in hostility toward God. It is time for you to live in true freedom.

True Freedom

There is no way I could write a book about spiritual bondage and slavery without writing about freedom. It does no good to identify a problem without providing a solution. Hope is found in showing others the way out of their situations.

I hear people say they are free, but I oftentimes wonder how they define freedom. Freedom has become an overly used word in our society. I do agree that freedom is a great thing. It is better to be liberated than it is to be confined. However, the Christ follower is both free and restrained. We are free in Christ to move and walk outside of the walls of religious restraint; however, such freedom does not grant us the right to live sinful, reckless lives.

The very idea of freedom can become bondage to someone who does not clearly understand it. Too much freedom places people in bondage to their own vices and weaknesses. They think up what is right then carry it out however they choose to do so. They do whatever they would like when they would like to do it. They are led by their own passions, wants and desires. What they do not realize is their idea of freedom is reckless and dangerous. This should not be the reality for a

Christ follower. Although we are not constrained to many religious obligations, we should not think that it is okay to live our lives in complete rebellion. We should still continue to strive towards holiness in all we do and say. Our lives should be a model for others to live by. We should be committed to doing what is right even if we do not feel like it. Our feelings should never push us to do something that would dishonor God or our parents—even if we feel as though they dishonor us.

Holiness is still the standard for Christ followers, and we should strive to attain it in every way. The standard of holiness draws a clear line and defines what is and is not honorable towards God. For example, just because people say you have the freedom to sleep with as many people as you want does not mean it is what you are supposed to do. Sleeping around is not honorable to God or your body. The use of freedom in that situation is perverse and the outcome will be perversion. It would be better for the person to be thrown in jail than for them to be mentally handicapped by their perverse idea of freedom.

We must not forget that freedom means we are set free from bondage. The most common bondage for a believer is sin. Its grip is tight and damning, but Christ sets us free from it. He also sets us free from sin's eternal consequences, from hopelessness, from despair and ultimately, from eternal death. Our freedom in Christ means that we are able to deny the old deeds of the flesh and live above the ways of this world. We are capable of standing firm in the face of sin without being moved or shaken by it. Therefore, if you have been set free do not be burdened again by the yoke of slavery.

THE GOSPEL

I know the bondage of sin is real because, like you have read, I have been in it. This is what made the Gospel such a liberating message for me. It was like I was sitting in a jail cell being tormented and tortured by sin. My perverse way of thinking represented the iron bars that kept me imprisoned. I had moments where I felt like I was free, but those moments were short-lived. In fact, the cell got bigger, giving me the illusion that I was experiencing some sense of freedom. When I went to the doors to escape I was snatched back to my knees. I mourned and cried under the weight of sin because it was too heavy for me to carry. Then, I heard the Gospel message. I heard the good news about Jesus Christ setting me free from slavery and breaking the chains that held me in bondage. I heard the news about how others had been set free through Him. I knew I had to encounter Him. Once I believed in Him He transformed my entire life. He broke the chains that held me captive. He tore down the iron doors that kept me trapped. He lifted the weight of sin that sat on my back. He released me from my bondage.

He did a work I was not capable of doing on my own. He set me free to live in Him, not the world. The very life I knew was gone, and I was challenged to renew my mind in Him. I had to submit to Him so the Holy Spirit could work freely within me to bring about true change. He set me free from the bondage of sin. I am able to finally live without worry and care because I know I am firmly rooted in Him. I am able to not fear what man can do to me because I know I abide in Christ. I am set free. I am made whole. This is great news, is it not? It is news that is worth being shared all over the world. And this news means so much to me because I am aware of the bad news. I look back at my experience in that cell and I break down in tears of gratitude. Christ did not have to set me free, but He did. The least I can do is sacrifice and submit my life to Him. The same is true for you. I pray you experience this true freedom.

I also pray that it does not stop with you. What good is it to have good news and not share it? Good news is worth sharing because it gives true freedom to those who hear it. This is why the Gospel is commonly referred to as "Good News." It is worth sharing. Make sure you experience it for yourself, then be free to share it with others. This is true freedom. And agree with me right now that YOU are NOT FOR SALE! Believe it and live like it. Stay focused, and keep your eyes on eternity. It is all to Jesus we surrender! God bless you.